AVOID DANGER: THINK SAFETY FIRST!

<u>BE SAFE-R®</u>

By: Brenda Meadows Wallace

TABLE OF CONTENTS:

Chapter Nine: PERSONAL SAFETY, ENVIRONMENTAL SAFETY & CYBERSECURITY

ACKNOWLEDGEMENTS

WHAT IS BEING SAID ABOUT THIS BOOK?

PREFACE: WHY IS BRENDA WALLACE WRITING A SAFETY BOOK FOR YOU?

I NEVER EXPECTED TO WRITE A PERSONAL SAFETY BOOK! I am a positive, happy person and do not worry about things. My writing started at an early age. Safety awareness and self-defense came much later, as my life took on many turns and crossroads. These crossroads made me aware that change and dangers come and go. How we prepare ourselves in advance can make or break us. If we are prepared, we are not afraid and can face most obstacles, remain productive and win! That is why I said, "Yes!" when I was asked to write a continuing education course on safety! This is the resulting book.

Last year, our Chief Executive Officer and Director of Career Development for BALDWIN REALTORS®, INC. asked if I would consider writing a 3 Hour Continuing Education Course on REALTOR SAFETY. I accepted the challenge, and I have wrestled with internal personal feelings and memories of what has sometimes happened to fellow REALTORS®. I received my first official Self Defense training in 2001. The Women's Council of REALTORS® and The Tuscaloosa Association of REALTORS® had sponsored a series of Self Defense training classes, and I found them to be empowering.

Dr. Sondra Lee, now an Oncology Certified Nurse Practitioner with a 5th Degree Black Belt in Isshinryu Karate, was our instructor. She and her husband have owned Karate studios for many years. She taught us avoidance techniques, confidence building and assertiveness exercises, escape techniques, combat exercises and practical safety. She had us share some stories, and she told us of other scenarios that could occur, and how to best handle them. All the time, she stressed that we had to know what we were capable of doing, and what we were not capable of doing. Each person has different physical and psychological strengths and weaknesses. Different tools work well for some people, and not well at all for others. The course by Dr. Sondra "Sandy" Lee, of Team Lee Studios, was empowering and life changing.

For this book, I am drawing upon personal experiences, those of others in real estate, my husband's Special Forces training in Escape and Evasion, Dr. Sondra Lee's training courses in personal self-defense, and some interaction with a very gifted grandson, who earned his silver medal in the National Karate Junior Olympics. That gifted grandson is now a Fire Chief, trained as a Paramedic and Hazardous Material expert and in Homeland Security rescue. I hope some of these experiences and safety tips help you decide to make the time to become SAFE-R®!

INTRODUCTION:

AFTER READING THIS BOOK, I PROMISE YOU CAN HAVE A PLAN FOR SAFETY AS THOROUGH AS YOUR PLAN FOR SUCCESS!

If you have a successful Real Estate Career or just think you may want one, this book is for you. I promise to give you relevant information to help formulate your plan for safety as thoroughly as your plan for success! This behind the scenes view, different from what you normally see about real estate, will help you stay SAFE-R® and be more successful! Success and Safety require advanced thorough planning. The similarities involve visualizing, knowledgeable planning, setting boundaries, setting goals and being assertive about the things that are important to you. If you want to change your life, or improve your life, this book is for you!

In this book, I promise to provide some personal stories that will help you see the important reasons for forming your SAFE-R® habits. You can be very happy and successful in real estate if you set boundaries and have a plan for your career! After thirty successful years in real estate, it is time for me to share an inside look at our profession. Having been the recipient of an International Real Estate Franchise Sales and Customer Service Award, and having trained hundreds of REALTORS®, I built a successful and was excited to know she had launched a new career. She was married to a physician, and her brother was in law-enforcement. She had selected a well-respected and strong real estate company, with security measures in place to help keep their real estate agents safe. A few years earlier, a REALTOR® had been murdered about 50 miles away, by someone travelling through this town before reaching Birmingham, Alabama. Though it had been several years, everyone still maintained rigid adherence to safety procedures in this office. She had explained this to her family. Everyone was pleased!

After entering the foyer and receiving a warm greeting, she was pleased to hear the phone ring and be told, "You have a buyer call on the line!" She could not be happier. This nice middle-aged man expressed a strong interest in seeing the inside of a lovely home in a great neighborhood, as soon as possible. As luck would have it, the property was vacant, and could be shown immediately! According to protocol, she gave the address of the property to the secretary and the name of the buyer. It was a beautiful day, and it would be perfect if this couple loved this home and wanted to buy it. There were several other homes she could show them, if she needed to show different houses.

As she pulled up to the home, the gentleman seemed nice and was anxious to see the inside. His wife was not with him; however, he seemed safe. Occupied homes were all around this one. Everything seemed to be acceptable downstairs, so they climbed the stairs to see the rest of the home. As she stepped in the upstairs bathroom, something changed. He blocked the entrance and became aggressive. A fight began, and the cell phone flew from her hand, automatically dialing her mother. Her mother answered the phone and heard her daughter's distressed screams. She did not know where her daughter was, and she felt helpless. She did remember her daughter had told her about the real estate office having security procedures to help protect her. She immediately called and asked them to please help her daughter! The secretary sprang into emergency mode, rapidly alerting the Qualifying Broker and the Police Department. The Qualifying Broker and his Commercial Real Estate Broker jumped in the car and headed for the address that had been left by the new REALTOR®. They arrived before the police, and found her alive, alone, and severely traumatized. The man had sexually assaulted her at knife point and threw her clothes into the commode.

This REALTOR® was a very strong lady, and she was alive. She gave me permission to tell her story because she does not want anyone else to think that danger cannot find them. A small town, strong family support and even safety procedures are NOT a GUARANTEE that you will be safe. She gave a description of the assailant, and with the support of her family, friends, police department and medical support, she spoke to our Association of REALTORS® that year. She said, "He is not robbing me of anything else. I will be successful, and I will have a life!" She has gone on to have a wonderful family and successful career. This was not an easy task. She decided she would not let him destroy her life.

I was told of a former special forces soldier, who met someone to show a land parcel, and went missing. He was found in a shallow grave. The alleged buyer had shot him and tried to hide the evidence. Recently, the National Association of REALTORS® notified our membership of the death of a young family man, who was killed at an Open House. Though these incidents are rare, they occur much too often. I live in one of the safest areas in the United States; yet, we have seen an increase in people calling for an appointment to see a home, and then they will try to steal pharmaceuticals or other valuable items. Recently, a female prospect attacked a male REALTOR® at an Open House because he tried to stop her from stealing prescription medications from the bathroom in this occupied home. She got away from the REALTOR® but was apprehended by the police within a short distance of the home.

Law enforcement officers tell us that the introduction of illegal drug trafficking, gang activities, and human trafficking, have made their way into all areas of the world. Once quiet cities are no longer exempt. We must be aware that any place is connected via the internet and interstate highways. There is no guarantee of safety. Life always has uncertainties; however, there are many things we can do to lessen the chances of our being harmed.

What can we do to lessen the possibility that we will encounter someone intending to harm us? We have had police departments, hazardous material experts, homeland security experts and self-defense instructors actively support REALTOR® SAFETY.

Though safety is not guaranteed, our chances are greatly increased if we know certain proven principles for staying safe.

Chapter Two

BE SAFE-R®: BE AWARE, AVOID DANGER, ESCAPE & SURVIVE!

I received basic danger avoidance training when hired as a Manager for OLSTEN PERSONNEL SERVICES. We corporate called on all major corporations within the cities we served. That meant, this age 20 something version of me, was going alone to call on industrial clients, the civic center, manufacturing facilities and all sizes of corporations. My training was in major cities: Westbury, NY, Newark, NJ, Houston, TX, Nashville and Memphis, Tennessee and Birmingham, Alabama. Later, as a Management Consultant and Corporate Trainer for CENTURY 21 CORPORATION, I traveled alone and called on offices across Alabama, Mississippi, Tennessee and the Florida Panhandle. This often meant being on the road and arriving in strange cities at night. This did not totally prepare me for some of the *seemingly safe* encounters in selling real estate. I had a lot to learn about misjudging people, and about not being assertive enough.

In 2001, the Tuscaloosa Association of Realtors® and the Women's Council of Realtors® worked together to procure Safety Training for our membership. Since that time, I have been a strong believer in the power of being AWARE, and of learning AVOIDANCE & ESCAPE techniques.

LET'S BEGIN BY STATING THESE RULES ARE INTENDED FOR YOUR INCREASED AWARENESS! I AM A REALTOR®, NOT A SELF DEFENSE EXPERT. YOU SHOULD SEEK PROFESSIONAL PERSONAL TRAINING IN SELF DEFENSE FROM SOMEONE WHO UNDERSTANDS YOUR STRENGTHS AND LIMITATIONS. THIS BOOK IS NOT INTENDED TO BE A REPLACEMENT FOR PROFESSIONAL TRAINING.

RULES TO HELP US STAY SAFE-R®:

1. Take a personal defense course from a Certified Professional. This should be someone, who knows your physical & psychological strengths and weaknesses! Practice basic Avoidance & Escape in the classroom, and it will be easier to remember on and off your job.

2. Realize that danger is a possibility, and you must be knowledgeable.

3. B aware of your surroundings: Look, Listen and Be Alert.

4. Do not meet people alone when you do not know them.

5. Wear comfortable conservative clothes. Do not carry a large amount of cash or wear expensive jewelry.

6. Never park so that your car is blocked from a quick exit, and make sure your car is parked to draw attention of the neighbors.

7. Remember, you are safer working in a team.

8. Meet people you do not know at your office or in a public place where you know other people, and there are security cameras. Be sure there is a photo of the person and their license registration plate on the vehicle. Use your camera on the cell phone if you need it! Many REALTORS® ask to scan or photograph their Driver's License.

9. Always have the customer or client walk ahead of you & do not allow them to be between you and the exit from the room and house.

10. Do not let someone you do not know get too close. Keep out of their reach & keep them in your view. Keep a car, table or chair between you and a possible attacker.

11. Always lock your car doors when you leave the car & when you get back in the car.

12. Before getting in your car, look inside to make certain no one is hiding in the floor of back seat.

13. Do not park next to panel trucks since most abductions occur from that type or similar vehicle.

14. If someone is just sitting in a vehicle next to where you are parked…Be aware, especially if they are on the side nearest you. It is better to return to the store ,or other place of business, and have a guard or manager walk you to the car as a precaution.

15. If something does not look right at a property you are showing, or any other location, always walk away and have someone accompany you.

16. If you are in a locked car and you realize there are people loitering near you, keep the doors locked and move to a safer place.

17. When you come out of the bank, store, etc., always lock your doors and do not just sit there and balance your account. Do not be distracted and vulnerable to attack.

18. If someone ever successfully hides in your car and pulls a gun, do not let them talk you into going with

them. ESCAPE! If they say you will be safe if you drive them to where they say, do not believe them!

19. If you need to escape from someone who has gotten in your car and pointed a gun at you, get out and RUN! If your car is moving when you see them, one recommendation of policemen has been to speed up and crash into something to deploy your airbag, even a police car! Get out of the car and run toward other people. If they have hidden in your car or jumped in your stopped vehicle with a gun, they probably did not take time to put on a safety belt and will most likely be hurt or stunned worse than you.

20. Keep in mind that someone with a pistol, is probably not accurate when shooting at a moving target.

21. It is said that you are more likely to survive a wound to the right side of your body, than your left. If up close and eminent, try to move or knock the gun away from your left side.

22. When you are showing a home, make sure you can easily and

quickly get back out the exit. Leave the door unlocked, unless you feel the outside is less safe than the inside of the home. Make lots of noise if you must escape. Scream and use your emergency alert on your car key to draw attention!

23. Avoid showing homes after dark. If you must show someone you know after dark, it is better to have someone go with you, and still follow all safety rules.

24. If you are showing a home after dark: Have on interior lights and all blinds and curtains open.

25. If you are stopped by a police car on a private stretch of road, keep your engine running and do not roll down your window except an inch or two. Tell them you have been instructed by your company not to get out of your vehicle until you follow them to the police station. This is acceptable behavior. Do not be intimidated. Be courteous, respectful, and careful. Some criminals pose as a law enforcement officer.

26. If you become aware you are in an unsafe situation, leave

immediately. Keep your doors locked and call 911.

27. Have voice controlled emergency systems and direct dial emergency numbers on your telephone. Do not forget to have your complete emergency information, including your medical, in your telephone and listed with your office and personal emergency contacts. Be certain to include a current photo and vehicle identification information.

28. If you have small children, have them trained in safety techniques. A nurse and Karate Instructor trained her small children to get underneath her parked car, when she gave a certain safety alert signal. If Mom had to eliminate the threat from a bad person, they were to get underneath the car and stay there until Mom said they could safely come out.

29. It is good business to provide a safety information brochure for your seller clients. Some possible examples: Clients should never leave prescription medications, small valuables and/or jewelry out when their home is being shown. Clients should not allow people

inside their home for alleged showings. You or another real estate person will schedule appointments and show the home. NEVER leave out firearms or other dangerous items. Children will be entering their homes, and sometimes slip away from their guardian.

30. It is good business to provide a safety information brochure for your buyer clients. Some possible examples: Be aware that homes may contain items that may be harmful to your health and have not been put away by the owner. Be aware that this area may have some insects, or other natural pests, which may be hazardous to your health. Please avoid swimming pools and play areas which might pose a hazard to your child, or other family member. Do not walk over land or vacant properties without a REALTOR® who has scheduled an appointment and will accompany you.

31. Dr. Sondra "Sandi" Lee, of Tuscaloosa County, Alabama, who taught my first Self Defense Course, taught us many avoidance skills and methods of dealing with

attackers, and provided input on various defense tools that work for different people. I would like for you to take a Self Defense course equally thorough. I cannot stress the importance of learning from an expert. Practice with your Self Defense Coach the techniques they feel would work best for your physical and psychological strengths and weaknesses! Some things she had us practice included the following:

If someone gets too close and starts to grab you around the neck from behind, remember to keep your chin down to avoid their being able to choke you unconscious, and try to angle your chin toward the inside bend of their elbow for easier breathing until you can escape. Try to break loose or defend yourself by stomping their feet, pinching or clawing soft tissue, kicking and punching with your elbows and lower part of hand. Attack the vulnerable spots: eyes, nose, groin, and solar plexus. RUN TO GET AWAY TOWARD OTHER PEOPLE & SCREAM AND MAKE AS MUCH NOISE AS POSSIBLE!

If they grab your wrists, twist your hands forcefully toward their thumbs and out of their grip to break free. GET AWAY!

If they are holding your arms and you cannot break free, try going limp in order to use your weight as a weapon. Often this can break their hold and allow you to get away! Run and scream. Draw attention by making loud noise! Use your car alarm or other mechanical distress signal!

<u>This list is not intended to be everything you will learn in your personal and professional Self Defense Course. Be prepared, stay alive and thrive!</u>

Chapter Three

DON'T BE A "BABY DOE" IN THE HEADLIGHTS! STAY AWARE & ALIVE!

We all are distracted by events in our daily lives. That is no secret. We know that looking at our cell phone while driving causes accidents! Distracted driving is against the law in many states. Looking at our cell phones while walking can prove to be dangerous. Criminals look for easy targets, especially people who are not paying attention to their surroundings. AT ALL TIMES, we should be focused on where we are and what we are doing. To be safe, and to be successful, we must observe the people and things around us, and focus on the present. Do not let your mind wander to yesterday or tomorrow. Stay focused on what you are accomplishing now. You will be safer, and you will be more effective in your personal relationships and business relationships.

I had a friend tell me, just today, of pulling over to make a call in her home state. She was a REALTOR® in a large metropolitan midwestern city, and she needed to use her phone to make a business call. She was in a convertible and had the top up with the air conditioner running. Fortunately, she followed the smart path and left her engine running and remained observant of her surroundings. In her side mirror, she saw a young man of approximately fifteen years of age, approaching her car with a knife in his hand! She immediately placed her transmission in drive and put her foot on the gas pedal. Just as she began to accelerate, another car came from the far lane and pulled into her lane, as though trying to block her path. She successfully swerved and missed the car and continued to drive as fast as possible to a safer area, while calling the police. The police dispatched a car to her area and saw a young man with a severe cut and bleeding arm. He and his mother refused to allow him to receive treatment. The policemen noticed some other nearby young men who were acting suspicious. She was asked if anyone was bleeding when she saw the young man with the knife approaching her car. She assured them that she saw no one bleeding at the time. The person they described as bleeding, matched the description of her would-be assailant. The police said there had been gang activity in that area, and they believed the young man was trying to attack her as a part of gang initiation. When he failed his mission, they believed the other gang members retaliated by slashing his arm, and he was afraid to seek help at the hospital because he knew he would have to answer questions.

It is not uncommon following my REALTOR® Safety classes, to have students come forward after class and tell me of various "near misses" that have occurred in their careers. In addition to staying aware, we need to increase our knowledge base to recognize things that are not safe. If a person wants to see a home, it is appropriate to make certain someone is helping them with the prequalification for a loan. When they meet with a lender and have their credit report pulled, it is a much safer prospect, and their offer will be taken seriously by the seller of any property you find for them. If a person does not want to meet you at your office, get prequalified by a lender or be on camera, <u>perhaps you do not want to meet them at a vacant property on four acres!</u>

Beware of things that just do not make sense or feel right. If their story does not sound feasible, or they appear not to have taken a bath for the past week, get the help of your Real Estate Managing Broker or Sales Manager. Serious buyers take baths! Trust me, their car did not break down a couple of miles from your office. I have worked with people who came straight from their construction jobs on stabilizing methane gas wells, and they often worked in muddy, hot conditions up to eighty hours a week, and there is a difference! Daily dirt is different.

Sometimes, you will trust a prospect or client, and everything seems fine. Perhaps, they were referred by another real estate company or Relocation Management Company. That does not mean it is alright for you to begin breaking your safety rules and taking chances. Boundaries are important! Do not let anyone pressure you into anything or any situation that does not feel right. Follow that instinctive safety warning. Also, realize that sometimes "friendly" strangers may fool you. Some people are very professional con artists. Rely on your office Safety Guidelines, and always be SAFE-R®! Do not break your safety rules for anyone. Stay aware! Observe any change in behavior.

A real estate broker in a quiet college town had a prospect walk in the office at closing time. The sun was setting, and it was a beautiful day! The prospect wanted to begin seeing homes that evening and the Broker explained that he did not assign agents to show homes to new clients in the evenings. He explained that he would be happy to assign an agent to meet with him the next morning, when the staff were available to help with setting up multiple showings, and he could better see the areas near the homes. In thirty minutes, it would be too dark to see the beauty of the neighborhoods.

The same man approached another qualifying broker, and he said it was too late that evening; however, he would provide a complementary room at the hotel next door to his office. The next morning, the prospective customer had left town. He did leave him a sizable meal and beverage bill to pay, along with his room charges.

In a nearby metropolitan city, the same man walks into a large real estate company and asks to see homes that day. He wants to see homes until he finds just the one home that he wants to buy. The conservative and experienced REALTOR® began showing him homes, and nothing seemed inappropriate. She showed several homes and checked in with her office, as she always did. She made her call to her husband, as she often did. She made certain she called regularly. Though, perhaps, something did not feel exactly right, she increased her check-in calls and continued working. At the end of the day, nothing unusual had occurred and she was ready to show her last home located just outside the metropolitan area, in a more private location.

The customer had been waiting for her to be tired and isolated. He attacked her, robbed her, and took her life. She left a husband, loving family, friends, and many REALTORS®, who realized she had done her job thoroughly and did nothing they had not done on every day of the year! Fortunately, the man was captured out of state by using her credit card. He died in jail.

Safety Awareness guidelines were strengthened even more. This was almost unheard of thirty years ago! Unfortunately, today more REALTOR® lives are being lost. We must go beyond our past layer of safety and create a greater awareness within the Real Estate Community. Many showing applications now include safety warning alerts that go out to our office if we do not check in within a certain number of minutes. Our local, state and National Association of REALTORS® are on full alert. Grants are being offered for new and better Agent Safety Training. Each of us is being more vigilant about looking out for other REALTORS® and volunteering to accompany them, if needed. Mortgage companies are pairing up with REALTORS® and many police departments are requesting we notify them immediately if we become aware of a possible threat. They had rather check out a false alarm than lose a member of our REALTOR® community.

Chapter Four

LEARN TO SAY "NO!'

Often, we are too anxious to be accommodating! Common techniques used by intruders, or kidnappers, are aimed at a person's compassionate nature. They may claim they need help doing something because of an alleged health problem, claim they need to come inside and use your restroom, claim they need help finding their lost dog, claim they need to use your telephone, claim they are in danger and need to get your help. Do not let someone you do not know through your locked door and do not follow them into an unknown space! It is acceptable to say "NO!"

Sometimes, the con artists claim they want to protect you. Though the person seems helpful and protective, if what they are offering to help with is against your rule, do not do it! Follow your own rules for the Safety Boundaries you know are right. When you are frightened or tired, it is easy to be gullible. Trust your brain over your emotions! Always think logically about the best course of action.

I was recently meeting two other real estate instructors before dawn. We wanted to travel together to an out of town meeting, and I was not familiar with the Interstate Exit recommended for leaving my car.

As I parked my car to go inside and speak with the gasoline station's manager, a man was helpful and held my door open and seemed very nice. Since I was approaching the location from a different highway, I asked if he could confirm the Exit number. He said I was correct. It was very foggy outside and still dark. I had been told to park on the vacant lot across the highway where many local people parked to commute. You could not even see the lot, or an entrance to it. Traffic was quite heavy. The manager of the gasoline service station confirmed that many people parked in the vacant lot across the road. I explained that it was so dark and foggy, I could not see an entrance way. Since I was filling up with gasoline and buying snacks, I asked if I might be permitted to park at the back side of her parking lot. She said her regional manager did not allow that. She did feel badly about it, since traffic was unusually busy, and the weather was bad. She said she hated for me to have to cross that busy street to get back over to the station to meet my instructor friends. The nice man who had held the door opened said, "Lady, that road is much too busy and visibility much too bad for you to be parking over there and then walking across the road to this service station. If you don't mind riding in my dirty truck, I can follow you over to the lot, and drive you back over here in my truck."

I did not want to inconvenience my friends, and it was frightening to park my car off the road where I could see nothing about the terrain. Perhaps, he could lead the way over there since his truck probably had brighter lights and he was probably familiar with the vacant lot. I did not want to wreck my car and I did not want to try to cross the busy road at night in a black pant suit. The fog was so thick, it was possible no one would see me, and I might be killed. This sounded like a good idea though I did not know the man. He seemed nice. I am usually a good judge of character.

Immediately, I thought about my rules and boundaries. You do not get into a car with someone you do not know. You always let someone know who you are with and where you are. You never go alone at night into a vacant area with strangers. How often had I heard news stories of people being killed by trusting someone who offered help! Always, I had said, "Oh my, that was not a smart thing for them to do!" Now, I had almost done the same thing.

Thanking the man for being so kind and helpful, I said, "I do not want to inconvenience you! My friends can just pick me up here and maybe it will be daylight in a few minutes when they arrive. I can call and let them know of the change in plans. They will not mind."

The man left the store, and the lady manager said, "You know, you are about my mother's age. I would not want her parking over there and crossing that busy street on foot, especially in this weather. My regional manager is not scheduled to be here, today. You can go ahead and park at the back of my parking lot." I thanked her and left a business card with her and inside my car windshield. I felt much better. Though he may have been safe, he may NOT HAVE BEEN SAFE! "AVOID DANGER: THINK SAFETY FIRST!"

In every Self Defense Awareness Class I teach, I do what my Self Defense Instructor had us practice. I have them shout, "NO!" This may seem unusual; however, being a very quiet nonassertive person in the past, I found this exercise to be liberating. It is OK to raise your voice and protest something that you do not want. It is OK to say "NO!" We practiced hitting a boxing bag while we screamed "NO!" <u>IT FELT GREAT!</u>

PART TWO: ENVIRONMENTAL & WILDLIFE RISKS

Chapter Five

AMERICA: THE BEAUTIFUL AND DANGEROUS

The United States is a beautiful country, filled with a variety of terrains and scenic wonders. We are fortunate to provide the opportunity for people to own a piece of the American Dream. We can spend our time seeing the most beautiful places in our area and showing the most beautiful homes, and we get paid for doing this! The people I have met in the last thirty-five years have been interesting and exciting. Many became some of my closest friends, and they sent their children and friends to me to buy their homes. Yet, every state has dangerous areas, too, and many people buy homes in proximity to wilderness areas. They love being near nature, and they love the excitement of the untamed wonders of the world! You cannot order wilderness properties, with beautiful wetlands, without getting the wildlife that inhabit those areas! If you do not like reptiles such as alligators, crocodiles or snakes, the wetland wilderness is not for you. Choose the areas that do not have wetlands. From shore to shore, we have a variety of flatlands, rolling hills, and spectacular mountains, and most all areas have snakes. When you enter their preferred environments, you may see them. Perhaps, that is why most people prefer to live in subdivisions and cities. Of course, snakes like city gardens, too! They often leave their low country when there are heavy rains, since they want a safe area, too. Homes that do not normally see snakes have reported them after heavy rains. My husband, the survivalist, tells me that snakes like to be in protected areas near their favorite food supplies. He reminds me of this just before I go to my blueberry bush!

As our country continues to grow, we are inhabiting more and more land that was previously used by wildlife. Because of this, we need to be knowledgeable of threats that are common to our area of the country. We should make certain that people do not go wandering alone across properties that we have listed for sale. Advise that they call for an appointment and have the property shown by a licensed REALTOR®, who is familiar with the property, local plants and animals. Try to find out from the sellers of the property if there are additional potential hazards. Something as simple as a large growth of poison ivy can make for a very uncomfortable prospect.

While showing a newly listed piece of land in a rural area of Alabama, near the site advertised for the construction of a new Mercedes Assembly Plant, my husband happened across an inground large cistern, used sometime in the past for the collection of rainwater. These can be very beneficial for watering crops or livestock; however, they should always have a safe lid in place. This was a large cistern with the lid left off! It had become inhabited by water moccasins! The lid was heavy and required a tractor to pull it in place, and this one had not been put back on. It was surrounded by high grass, and fortunately my husband saw it in time to steer the investor away from that area. These snakes are aggressive and very venomous.

There are mining pits for coal, or other minerals, which were never reclaimed and returned to their original condition. Often, they have filled up with water from underground streams or springs and have water moccasins. Other places with streams or wetlands are common habitats for several species of snakes. People have died by swimming in deserted pits, which sometimes look beautiful and are very deep. If bitten, they tend to panic and drown, or fail to make it to a hospital in time. Staying calm and getting immediate care is vital! The venom can be deadly and cause aggressive skin deterioration.

Across the United States, we have several varieties of venomous snakes that can be deadly. A good pair of snake boots and some safety training are recommended if you plan to show property. Many land sales agents use their all- terrain vehicles as much as possible. The knowledgeable outdoors enthusiasts know to avoid the wet low-lying areas and tall grassy areas; however, those are not the only areas snakes are seen. There are mountain snakes, too. Some of the more dangerous snakes in our nation are: Cottonmouth or Water Moccasin, Copperhead, Timber Rattlesnake, Black Diamond Rattlesnake, Eastern coral snake, Tiger Rattlesnake, Eastern Diamondback Rattlesnake, Mojave rattlesnake, Western Diamondback Rattlesnake, and Prairie Rattlesnake. They sometimes hide under logs or in thick grassy areas. You can find photos on Google or Wikipedia. While there, you can find other dangerous animals that will have you dialing Animal Control Numbers for your area or 911.

Copperhead snakes, coral snakes, water moccasins and rattle snakes have all been spotted on residential properties from time to time. Though snakes most often try to avoid humans, this is not always the case. The copperhead snake blends in easily with garden landscaping and has an extremely venomous bite. The bites most often occur when the snake is stepped on.

I was going for a walk in my subdivision, which was built near some wetlands and a ranch. As I was recognized by a new neighbor, she asked if I could maybe answer a question for her. "Is it true that some people have seen snakes in this neighborhood?" She said she had moved here from a larger city in another state and did not know much about wildlife or snakes. I told her that most subdivisions have snakes from time to time. Her lot backed up toward a large ranch and a pond, giving her a beautiful and tranquil view. She said she had a privacy fence, so would probably not have a problem! I asked if she had a dog, and she said she did. "Yes, I have a dog and it normally goes in and out through my pet door. I don't have my pet door installed at this time. I have just been leaving my back door open on pretty days so my dog can go in and out as he pleases! He is enjoying the large back yard." I told her that I did not know as much about snakes as my husband; however, I knew they could come into yards and to be sure she kept her grass cut and avoid high grass or thick plantings. Mentioning that once a snake had tried to get under a door where I worked across a street from a lake and warehouse, she said she thought she should go close her door. She has become a great neighbor, and I noticed she usually keeps her garage door closed, too!

Through the years, I have lived from Portland, Oregon to Ft. Lauderdale, Florida. The most feared animals are normally reptiles or bears, cougars, wolves, coyotes, wolverines and sharks. Scorpions and spiders are another extremely painful and sometimes deadly threat. The two most dreaded spiders are the black widow spider variety and the brown recluse spider, and sometimes we hear of Africanized "killer" bees. From sheer size of the animal, deer and bison can be very dreaded during their mating season. They become restless and aggressive and have crashed into moving cars. This collision can be deadly. Jellyfish can be extremely uncomfortable and wasps, yellow jackets and fire ants can cause serious pain and require medical attention. Sensitivity to the stings, can sometimes cause extreme swelling and pain. Many people do not recognize the signs of a fire ant mound, and this can cause them to step on it. This can mean a fast trip to the doctor or emergency room, instead of seeing homes with you…or a different REALTOR®.

I have been bitten by a spider while showing a riverfront home that had been vacant. It felt like a bee sting and I slapped the front of my leg. I continued showing properties until I wrote a contract for the new Mercedes engineer the next day. The contract was accepted, and he left feeling very happy. I had not let anyone know about the bite. When I checked it, the bite had caused a small hole and it was surrounded by a purple circle. I showed it to my husband, and he immediately drove me to the emergency room! I found out from a house painter, that he had waited too long to get treatment from a brown recluse bite and lost the underlying muscle in his arm. They are common spiders that often do not bite unless they are touched or mashed. They tend to hide in cool, dark places. Many spiders gravitate toward water. Other favorite places are the inside of closets and drawers. Many people are bitten when they put on clothing without checking them. They have been known to hide in socks, gloves, shoes and on the underneath side of a commode seat. Fortunately, I was taking antihistamines for respiratory allergies, and the doctor felt that had probably helped! He filled me full of antihistamine, anti-inflammatory and antibiotic! He said they normally saw that severe reaction from a black widow or brown recluse, and he thought it had probably been a brown recluse. Fortunately, I healed quickly and without a scar. Now, I have read that black widows can be more poisonous than a snake, with severe stomach pains, body aches, and even passing out. Immediate care can be a matter of life and death.

Showing homes throughout the United States is a pleasant experience! Rarely do we encounter problems. Being prepared can make a big difference for ourselves and our clients. Just as we know when a storm is coming, we learn when certain properties present a greater risk, and I always suggest having a personal first aid kit in your car. Out west in higher altitudes, a hot summer day can turn quickly to an unexpected snowstorm, and most people keep warm clothing, a blanket and food in their vehicle when driving through the mountains. Along the sunny southeastern coastline, we can quickly have a heat generated thunderstorm, so we carry an umbrella in our cars. There is a possibility of earthquakes on our California coastline, so we have emergency supplies in our cars, homes and offices. You can be SAFE-R® by advanced planning and being aware! Most days are exciting and wonderful, and the other days are manageable opportunities for service.

Chapter Six

TERRORISM & CATASTROPHIC EVENTS: HOW DO YOU AVOID OR STOP THEM?

On August 5, 2019, the Federal Bureau of Investigations Director announced a surge in hate crimes. In schools, malls and workplaces, they are seeing as many as thirty cases a year. Within twenty-four hours, we had two mass murders this past weekend of August 4th. El Paso, Texas has reported 20 killed and 26 injured in a Walmart store. The killer had left his hate-filled manifesto. In Dayton, Ohio, 9 were killed, including the suspected gunman's sister, and 27 injured. Some reports alleged a "Sexual Assault List" and a "Kill List". What can be done? I remember spending time in each of those cities during my years of travel and enjoying their normal and pleasant way of life!

According to mental health and governmental law enforcement organizations, in advance of incidents, there are often clues available. Sometimes, those clues are online social media rants. Other times, family or acquaintances have observed tendencies toward violence and a lack of guilt for their actions. Some people are afraid to notify the authorities and others say they are shocked into an inability to speak up. Whether hate or bigotry, mental illness, or crimes fueled by drugs, or the illicit drug trafficking, human trafficking or illegal weapon sales: we must find a way to eliminate this rise in crime. For now, how do we help solve the problem? How do we avoid being a victim?

Authorities have asked us to report signs of dangers. Whether, we see a box or bag that is left unattended in a public place, or we hear the online rants of someone wanting to kill anyone who has a different lifestyle or opinion, an early report could stop untold deaths by bombs or assault weapons. As REALTORS®, we are constantly in public settings and private settings where no one else is with us. We must become more aware of potential dangers and be able to safely leave the scene and call 911. The law enforcement agencies are saying it is much better to call in a possible threatening situation that proves to be harmless, than to ignore it and have you, your family, clients are large numbers of our citizens harmed or killed.

Many possible solutions have been offered from eliminating videos or other media depicting gruesome violent actions to more law enforcement and improved mental health care. Until solutions can be found, we must be aware of the unlikely, yet possible, dangers. What is suggested if we find ourselves in this situation? Again, a great Self Defense and safety course is strongly advised. Many schools and employers are advising to ESCAPE or HIDE IN PLACE & CALL FOR HELP. Some qualified civilian heroes have managed to eliminate, or at least control, the damages of an otherwise catastrophic event. This is an area outside my experience; however, I do want you to discuss the possibilities and be aware of your safest possible responses for you and those you love.

Chapter Seven

HOW TO AVOID POSSIBLE DRUG PROPERTIES? OTHER CRIME SCENES?

In the past ten years, Police and Sheriff Departments have asked us to be on guard to avoid walking into an illegal drug environment. There is no area of the country remote enough to remove it from possible drug and gang traffic finding them over the internet, interstate highways, or coastlines! Human trafficking is now throughout the world, including the United States. Children and adults have been targeted. We must increase our awareness of danger and have an established Safety Plan that is as well planned as our business plan. What are some signs of danger?

1. Be aware of chemical scents or unexpected people at vacant properties, especially those properties that are remote. These properties may be targeted and used for the manufacture of methamphetamines. Do not enter the building. Leave and call 911. Our law enforcement officials had rather make an unnecessary call than have us harmed.

2. Know that Marijuana, Cocaine, Heroin, Methamphetamines, Fentanyl, Carfentanil, dangerous new synthetic drugs such as Spice, and illegally acquired prescription drugs are a national problem covering our

entire country. This causes death, violence and increased crime.

3. Methamphetamines and Fentanyl can be absorbed through your skin. If you suspect drugs have been manufactured in a house, or there are drugs or drug making items such as tubing, trays, aerosol cans and strange chemical odors, do not enter the property and call your local police or sheriff department. Fentanyl may cause an overdose within a matter of minutes, resulting in immediate death. Fentanyl effects are magnified by the presence of other drugs or alcohol in your body.

4. According to the Federal Drug Enforcement Agency, Fentanyl is 80-100% stronger than morphine. Medical News Today reported, "Fentanyl is roughly 100 times more potent than morphine and 50 times more potent than heroin. In fact, it is the most potent opioid pain reliever available for us in medical treatment..." "Accidental deaths are increasingly common." "The difference between a therapeutic dose and a deadly dose of fentanyl is very small. There are many illegal analogs and derivatives of fentanyl that are much stronger than the prescription version." See article: medicalnewstoday.com

5. According to justthinktwice.gov "Carfentanil is a dangerous new factor in

the nation's opioid crisis. This drug is behind rashes of deadly overdoses.... a white powdery substance that looks like it could be cocaine or heroin. Drug dealers mix it with heroin to presumably make the heroin stronger. It is 10,000 times more potent than morphine and 100 times more potent than fentanyl. The drug is also used to tranquilize elephants.... This drug is so powerful it poses a significant threat to first responders and law enforcement personnel who touch it by accident. In addition, people can overdose on carfentanil quickly. Multiple doses of the anti-overdose drug Narcan may not be effective. Users exposed to carfentanil can experience dizziness, clammy skin, shallow breathing, heart failure and more." (REALTORS®, DO NOT TOUCH THIS & LEAVE THE PROPERTY IMMEDIATELY!)

SAFETY ALERT from the Federal Drug Enforcement Agency: "Carfentanil: A Dangerous New Factor in the U.S. Opioid Crisis"

Officer & Public Safety Information:
"Carfentanil and other fentanyl analogues present a serious risk to public safety, first responder, medical, treatment, and laboratory personnel. These substances can come in several forms, including powder, blotter paper, tablets,

patch and spray. Some forms can be absorbed through the skin or accidentally inhaled. If encountered, responding personnel should do the following based on the specific situation.

Exercise extreme caution. Only properly trained and outfitted law enforcement professional should handle any substance suspected to contain fentanyl or a fentanyl-related compound. If encountered, contact the appropriate officials within your agency.

Be aware of any sign of exposure. Symptoms include respiratory depression or arrest, drowsiness, disorientation, sedation, pinpoint pupils, and clammy skin. The onset of these symptoms usually occurs within minutes of exposure.

Seek IMMEDIATE medical attention. Carfentanil and other fentanyl-related substances can work very quickly, so in cases of suspected exposure, it is important to call EMS immediately. If inhaled, move the victim to fresh air. If ingested and the victim is conscious, wash out the victim's eyes and mouth with cool water.

Be ready to administer naloxone in the event of exposure. Naloxone is an antidote for opioid overdose. Immediately administering naloxone can reverse an overdose of carfentanil, fentanyl, or other opioids, although multiple doses of naloxone may be required. Continue to administer a dose of naloxone every 2-3 minutes until the individual is breathing on his/her own for at least 15 minutes or until EMS arrives.

Remember that carfentanil can resemble powdered cocaine or heroin. If you suspect the presence of carfentanil or any synthetic opioid, do not take samples or otherwise disturb the substance, as this could lead to accidental exposure. Rather, secure the substance and follow approved transportation procedures.

Lethality: Carfentanil is used as a tranquilizing agent for elephants. The lethal dose range for carfentanil in humans is unknown; however, carfentanil is approximately 100 more times more potent than fentanyl, which can be lethal at the 2-miligram range, depending on route of administration and other factors." (See Photos at: dea.gov)

6. When drug dealers or manufacturers have taken over a property, they sometimes plant explosives that will go off when doors are opened, or light switches turned on. DO NOT ENTER!

7. Prior to the newer line of even deadlier drugs, Sheriff Ted Sexton, Tuscaloosa County, Alabama, said when his men were

accidentally exposed to Meth or other illicit drugs, they were stripping down and washing all over in Dawn to lessen any potential effects of the drug being absorbed through their skin. NOTE: THIS NEW LINE OF ILLICIT DRUG IS EVEN MORE DANGEROUS!

My friend's EMT son was interested in buying a home through me. We had his preapproval for financing and began searching for his first home! I received a call from him requesting that I show a four- bedroom home in a very nice neighborhood. The price was much lower than the normal price for the neighborhood. He was my Buyer Client, and I explained to him that when a house was that much lower than the competition, something was probably very wrong. He said he did not mind putting work in the home and creating some sweat equity. He was excited!

The home showed vacant in the Multiple Listing Service and I met his mother and him at the home. There was furniture stacked out back, and there was a lockbox on the front door. The note in the Multiple Listing Service said the home had been repossessed. We entered the home and immediately knew it had been abused. The carpet had filthy unidentifiable stains, smoke debris was hanging from the ceiling, and the smell was toxic! He kept thinking he could clean it up because it was the most house that he had seen in that price range. We were there about an hour. That evening, I had a splitting headache.

My phone was ringing early the next day, and I still had the headache. It was my EMT client on the line, "Miss Brenda, I had an awful headache after being in that home yesterday!" I said I did, too. "In fact, my head is still hurting. I am wondering if perhaps meth was cooked in that house! The Sheriff spoke to us at a REALTOR® luncheon, and told us it was happening in our area, and to please be careful." He said that he would see what he might be able to find out from some friends in the police department.

It wasn't long until my telephone rang with his number on Caller I.D. "Miss Brenda, I checked on that house and my Police friends said the people had been arrested on Meth manufacturing charges!" That home was eliminated; however, my headache was not.

My grandson was a Hazardous Material Specialist and a Paramedic with a Florida Fire Department, and I decided to call him for more information. I told him that my client and I had both been in a house where Meth had been manufactured and that we both had a splitting headache! He said, "Grandma, you should not go in a property where Meth has been manufactured unless you have on HazMat Gear! That can be absorbed into the sheetrock and other building materials, and you can accidentally get it into your system! That is very dangerous!" He said that sometimes, concentration was so high in a house that it had to be torn down and removed, and one home even had the soil removed for clean up before a new home was built. I told him nothing had been reported by the bank that had foreclosed on the property.

We must be more vigilant at protecting ourselves and our clients through improved policies and procedures. Other states are tracking this type of drug activity to protect their citizens. I was happy to hear that Georgia has enacted more stringent laws, too. HEALTH AND SAFETY IS TOO IMPORTANT TO ALLOW THIS TO AFFECT THE LIVES OF REALTORS® AND THEIR CLIENTS.

PART THREE: CYBERSECURITY

Chapter Eight

HOW SAFE ARE YOU & YOUR CLIENTS?

I am certain you have encountered Malware,
Computer Viruses or Hackers. It is no longer a shock
to hear of someone having seemingly endless
problems. We buy an Anti-Viral program from a
trusted company, perhaps we add an additional
Malware Product. Two weeks later, we are visiting
our favorite Internet Security Specialist! Or worse,
maybe you had your identity stolen. Fortunately, our
National Association of REALTORS®, State
Associations, and Local Association of REALTORS®
joined in that fight to help protect our national
membership! Everything is improving, yet everything
is different. We no longer accept any new person who
wants to be our Friend on Social Media sites. Now,
we must know them before accepting that new
invitation. You may even Cyber Stalk them to see if
they might be a legitimate potential client! Of course,

you never click on links in an email until you verify it is legitimate. More likely, even after you telephone your friend to see if she sent a link for you to get information you requested, you copy and paste it into your browser that has an additional security product!

Several years ago, some military leaders proposed that the greatest threat to the United States of America would be an Internet Threat targeting our Financial and Governmental sectors. Congratulations, that meant Banks, Real Estate Companies, and Title Companies would be fighting disruption of services and/or stolen information. Today, we have totally stopped emailing routing information for real estate closings of escrow. We do not even forward it from our Title Attorney to our client. We have been told that "someone is possibly hiding within your system waiting for an opportunity to pounce on your transaction and steal your clients' money!" Sadly, we have examples of exactly that occurring.

Let's review some of our new rules and practices for staying SAFE-R® with our computers and iPhones or Androids:

- Don't be the weak link!

- Keep Computer Software Updated

- Keep your Internet Connection Secure with updates to Internet Modems & Routers

- Do not transmit any confidential information by standard email.

- Be cautious about what you send through encrypted email. How good is the encryption?

- Beware Phishing Scams. Yes, I know they look like your real supplier's mail!

- Warn Clients of Wire Fraud Possibilities.

- Don't copy your clients' confidential information & forward by email.

- Avoid Unsecured Networks. Don't even trust an unsecured network at your Public Library.

- Consider Virtual Private Networks for your everyday email use.

- Do not assume it is safe because it is your smart phone. They can be hacked, too.

- Ask for help from your Association of REALTORS®!

- Ask for help from your Real Estate Company

- Marry someone in Cybersecurity. (This one is just to see if you are paying attention!)

- Beware of Pop-Ups!

- Use https: when you are browsing websites. The addition of the "s" indicates you will only accept a "Secure Internet Site". Be aware that once you are on the secure site, you may still click on a link that can take you away to an unsecure site. Stay aware and do no use sites that are not secure. Make certain your public website is a secure site. Many people are no longer visiting sites that do not offer secure browsing.

- According to our banking industry, credit cards are more secure than debit cards or checks. Savings accounts generally are hacked less frequently than their other bank accounts. However, when an email is hijacked immediately before a closing, the money does not go directly to your savings account if the Cybercriminal has convincingly sent a new routing number to his account instead of yours to the Closing Attorneys or Title Company handling the Escrow. Also, if you sent your routing number to any account by email, remember that is no longer secure if the email is not secure.

Why has this become so important? Because billions of dollars have been stolen on an annual basis.

It is essential for you to have a professional Internet Technology Company providing guidance. We have a rapidly changing environment where new scams are created minute by minute, with malware that enables someone to hack in and mimic the legitimate websites or email addresses. The good news for the telephone companies is, they are very needed, again! In the past, we were afraid to send a Fax to a business or client, because someone in their office might pick it up and read it or steal our information. Emails were the most secure method to communicate. Now, many offices have returned to Fax. Just a minute! How about that scanner that gets it ready to go through the fax machine? Is that not basically a computer? So, we block out the confidential part of the document and call them and give that information. If my tech guy wasn't 20 something, I would think he was paranoid and senile!

When I first began having computer problems, I know all my friends thought I had finally read one book too many! Then, their corporations began having the same problems. When I spoke to a brilliant young man in the big box computer store, he said "I know I am appearing paranoid to some people, because I see everyone's computer problems!" Another told me that he had some customers who bought a new computer, thinking their old computer just did not work right, and then they put it in the corner and refused to use it after the first month.

Thankfully, I have had several clients who specialized in Internet Technology, and they liked the fact that I still loved computers! They still connect us to the world and get our jobs done more efficiently. We have wonderful organizations standing behind us, and we must listen to them and follow their directions.

PART FOUR: SECURITY FEEDBACK

Chapter Nine

PERSONAL SAFETY, ENVIRONMENTAL SAFETY & CYBER SECURITY

I would like to say, "Thank You!" to the many people who have been willing to share their experiences and their training.

I met a man, recently, who said his wife came home and told him that she was told it was no longer advisable to hold Open Houses alone. He decided to go with her, as a quiet attendee. During the Open House, two young men came into the house, who were obviously not there to buy a house. He said that both he and his wife felt if she had been there alone, things could have gone very badly.

A friend and her husband recently went for a walk outside her small-town subdivision and encountered wild boars! A caretaker of the adjacent land approached and said he never walked the property without a gun, since there was a herd of the wild boars, and they could be hostile and very dangerous. This was totally unexpected to the new residents of the area.

Many subdivisions, at the edge of towns, have unexpected visitors! Various species from the adjacent wilderness or ranching areas of their state are known to wander into their subdivisions in search of food. Large eagles, hawks and owls have been known to fly off with small domestic pets. Caution is advised until you familiarize yourself with your new home areas.

In an Association of REALTOR(S) training session, we learned that in our county, an Escrow Title Company had recently received an email from the address of the Seller in their closing office stating that he needed to change his routing address for proceeds of the sale to a different account from what he had earlier provided. The Title Manger called the real estate agent out of the closing and told her about the email from her client. IMMEDIATELY, the REALTOR® said, "No, it is not from him. He hates emails and is not sending anything!" They verified with the client that he had not authorized any change and saved him from a Cybercriminal's stealing his entire proceeds from the sale of his home! It has become a common scheme of cybercriminals attacking both buyers and sellers to misroute their funds.

Always be safe! Think, Be Aware of your surroundings, Be Knowledgeable, and enjoy your life and successful career for a very long time! BE SAFE-R®

I hope this book has made your life easier. I want you to enjoy your career and stay SAFE-R®! Real Estate is a wonderful career, and it can bring you more fulfillment and joy than you can imagine! I have loved this road, and the people who made my life so much better. I know the next twenty years will be just as exciting.

ACKNOWLEDGEMENTS

Many people helped keep me safer throughout my life and mentored me as an author, personnel manager, REALTOR®, and corporate trainer. I cannot possibly name all of them, though they will never be forgotten!

In preparing me to write this book, I must thank the following outstanding people:

Sondra Lee, DNP, a dedicated Doctor of Nursing Practice in Oncology with a 5th Degree Black Belt in Isshinryu Karate, who continues to change lives. Thank you for the life-changing Self Defense course in 2001!

Mr. Al Current of The Olsten Corporation who saw my potential and mentored me in safe and effective corporate calling.

Mr. Gene Darke, Former Tennessee State Director and Corporate Trainer of CENTURY 21 Management Academy, who made mastering the many courses I needed to teach a rewarding and meaningful learning experience.

Mr. Fred Ulbricht, President and Founder, FIRST REAL ESTATE CORPORATION, who allowed me to brainstorm with him and share his wisdom. Working as his Director of Corporate Marketing was a magnificent learning experience, as I observed his wisdom in managing his employees and agents, while protecting his customers and clients.

Kathy Czukor, Broker/Owner, REALTY EXECUTIVES – TUSCALOOSA, who persuaded me to become an Instructor licensed by The Alabama Real Estate Commission.

The Alabama Real Estate Commission's Educational Staff, who tirelessly train and guide us as we strive to continuously improve our profession and protect the consumers in Alabama: Ryan Adair, David Bowen, Pam Oates, Julie Norris and Nancy Williamson. They have given me countless hours!

The National Association of REALTORS®, the Alabama Association of REALTORS®, the Tuscaloosa County Association of REALTORS®, and BALDWIN REALTORS, INC. have been phenomenal! How can I say "Thank You" enough to Sheila Dodson, Chief Executive Officer, and Allison Woodham, Communications Director for BALDWIN REALTORS, INC. for asking me to write a Continuing Educational Course on REALTOR® SAFETY? That path has led me down rewarding paths I never planned.

Anne Powell, Director of Agent Development, and my most recent dedicated mentor, has encouraged me to follow my dream and gave me the honor of teaching for ACADEMY OF REAL ESTATE. Her introduction to Chief Executive Officer Johnny Roberts, and President Daniel Dennis of ROBERTS BROTHERS, INC, a Berkshire Hathaway Affiliate. opened a door to a very supportive environment, where individuality is welcomed, excellence is expected, and a supportive family environment sees you through any unexpected life changes.

Grayson Glaze, JD, CCIM, CPM – Executive Director, Alabama Center for Real Estate, Culverhouse College of Business, University of Alabama. "How could my husband and I thank you enough for your friendship and support? You have provided constant words of encouragement, and your leadership is an inspiration."

Cherie Moman, Director of Education, Marketing & Communications at Alabama Center for Real Estate, Culverhouse College of Business, University of Alabama. "Cherie, you have provided encouragement and pushed me to complete this cherished and emotional project! Your unexpected Podcast interview on REAL ESTATE MATTERS, ACRE ExploRE, made that day one I will always cherish, and one that meant this work of love was really happening! I owe you a debt of gratitude that can never be repaid. Let's save some REALTOR® lives and keep them **SAFE-R®**!"

My husband, Jim Wallace, who patiently stood by me while I locked myself away for countless hours of study and writing. He was the real estate broker who turned away many inappropriate people who sometimes tried to place the REALTORS® at our office in danger. We always appreciated his protective and watchful style of management. He also gave me a wonderful family and a new consultant, our grandson, Steven Wallace, Fire Chief/Paramedic/Hazardous   Material

Technician/National Junior Olympics Silver Medal recipient in Karate, and lifelong protector.

My family, who taught me that prayer provided the greatest protection I could ever know, was definitely helpful.

WHAT IS BEING SAID ABOUT THIS BOOK?

My first person to see this manuscript, **<u>AVOID DANGER: THINK SAFETY FIRST! BE SAFE-R®!</u>**

"It is a page-turner! This safety information, and the stories that make it memorable and relatable, will become a constant companion guide for helping REALTORS® know how to better handle the challenges and opportunities of this profession. It should be read over and over until it becomes the catalyst for their permanent safety plan, that will keep them and those they love SAFE-R® on and off the job." LTC James J. Wallace, USA Special Forces (Ret.)

www.ingramcontent.com/pod-product-compliance
Lightning Source LLC
Chambersburg PA
CBHW020621220526
45463CB00006B/2643